Who's the Dupe? by Hannah Cowley

A FARCE. IN TWO ACTS. AS PERFORMED AT THE THEATRE-ROYAL, DRURY-LANE.

Hannah Cowley was born Hannah Parkhouse on March 14th, 1743, the daughter of Hannah (née Richards) and Philip Parkhouse, a bookseller in Tiverton, Devon.

As one might expect details of much of her life are scant and that of her early life almost non-existent.

However, we do know that she married Thomas Cowley and that the couple moved to London where Thomas worked as an official in the Stamp Office and as a part-time journalist.

Her career in the literary world seemed to happen rather late. It was whilst the couple were attending a play, thought to be sometime in late 1775, that Cowley was struck by a sudden necessity to write.

Her first play, a comedy called The Runaway was sent to the famed actor-manager, David Garrick. It was produced at his final season at the Drury Lane theatre on February 15th, 1776. It was a success. She wrote her next two plays, the farce, Who's the Dupe? and the tragedy, Albina, before the year was out.

Getting these two plays into production took much longer and involved a very public spat with her rival Hannah More over whether Cowley's works had been plagiarised by More.

Cowley wrote her most popular comedy in 1780; The Belle's Stratagem. It was staged at Covent Garden.

Her next play, The World as It Goes; or, a Party at Montpelier (the title was later changed to Second Thoughts Are Best) was unsuccessful, but she continued to write and there followed another seven plays; Which is the Man?; A Bold Stroke for a Husband; More Ways Than One; A School for Greybeards, or, The Mourning Bride; The Fate of Sparta, or, The Rival Kings; A Day in Turkey, or, The Russian Slaves and The Town Before You.

In 1801 Cowley published perhaps her greatest poetical work. A six-book epic "The Siege of Acre: An Epic Poem".

That same year Cowley retired to Tiverton in Devon, where she spent her remaining years out of the public spotlight whilst she quietly revised her plays.

Hannah Cowley died of liver failure on March 11th, 1809.

Index of Contents

ACT II

SCENE I.—An Apartment
SCENE II.—A Drawing Room
Hannah Cowley – A Short Biography
Hannah Cowley – A Concise Bibliography
Scenarios of Some of Her Plays

WHO'S THE DUPE?

ACT I

SCENE I.—The Park

Flower **GIRLS**, and several **PERSONS** passing.

1st GIRL
I vow I han't had a customer to-day. Summer is coming, and we shall be ruined.—When flowers are plenty, nobody will buy 'em.

2nd GIRL
Aye, very true—People talks of summer; but for my part, give me Christmas. In a hard frost, or a deep snow, who's drest without flowers and furs? Here's one of the captains.

[Enter **SANDFORD**.

Flowers, sir!

SANDFORD
I have no silver.

2nd GIRL
Bless your honour! I'll take gold.

SANDFORD
Indeed.

2ⁿᵈ GIRL
Here's hyacinths, and a sprig of myrtle.

SANDFORD
I'd rather have roses. What will you take for these?

[Pinching her cheek.

2ⁿᵈ GIRL
I can't sell them alone—the tree and the roses must go together.

[Enter **GRANGER**.

SANDFORD
Ah! Granger, by all that's fortunate. I wrote to you last night in Devonshire to hasten your return.

GRANGER
Then your letter and I jostled each other at two o'clock on this side Hounslow. My damn'd postilion—nodding, I suppose, over the charms of some Greasalinda—run against the letter-cart, tore off my hind wheel, and I was forced to mount his one-eyed hack, and, in that curious equipage, arrived at three this morning.

SANDFORD
But how has the negociation with your brother ended? Will he put you into a situation to—

GRANGER
Yes, to take a sweating with the Gentoos. He'll speak to Sir Jacob Jaghire to get me a commission in the East Indies—'and, you know, every body grows rich there—and then, you know, you're a soldier, you can fight.' [In a tone of mimicry.

SANDFORD
Well, what answer did you give him?

GRANGER
Yes, Sir Bobby, I can fight. [Mimicking.] But I can't grow rich upon the smell of gunpowder. Your true East India soldier is of a different genus from those who strewed Minden with Frenchmen, and must have as great a fecundity of character as a Dutch Burgo-master. Whilst his sword is in his hand, his pen must be in his cockade: he must be as expert at fractions as at assaults; to-day moving down ranks of soft beings, just risen from their embroidery; to-morrow selling pepper and beetle-nut: this hour a son of Mars, striding over heaps of slain; the next an auctioneer, knocking down chintz and calico to the best bidder.

SANDFORD
And thus your negociation ended?

GRANGER

Except that I was obliged to listen to some very wise dissertation about running out, as he calls it, 'Five thousand—enough for any younger son, but the Prodigal.' [Mimicking.] Really, Sandford, I can't see how I can help it. Jack Spiller, to be sure, had nine hundred—the poor fellow was honest; but he married a fine lady, so died insolvent. I had a few more accidents of the same kind; my captaincy cost a thousand; and the necessary expenses in America, with the distresses of my fellow soldiers, have swallowed the rest.

SANDFORD
Poor Granger! So, with a spirit to do honour to five thousand a year, thou art not worth five shillings.

GRANGER
C'est vrai. Should my affairs with Elizabeth be crossed, I am the most undone dog on earth.

SANDFORD
Now tell me honestly, is it Elizabeth, or the fortune, which is your object?

GRANGER
Why look'e, Sandford; I am not one of those sighing milksops, who could live in a cottage on love, or sit contentedly under a hedge and help my wife to knit stockings; but on the word of a soldier, I had rather marry Elizabeth Doiley with ten thousand pounds, than any other woman on earth with a hundred.

SANDFORD
And the woman must be very unreasonable, who would not be satisfied with such a distinction. But do you know that Elizabeth's father has taken the liberty to chuse a son-in-law without your permission?

GRANGER
Ha! a lover! That then is the secret she hinted, and which brought me so hastily to town. Who—what is he?

SANDFORD
Every thing that you are not.

GRANGER
There is such a mixture of jest and earnest—

SANDFORD
Upon my soul 'tis confoundedly serious. Since they became my neighbours in Suffolk, I am in the secrets of the whole family, and, for your sake, have cultivated an intimacy with Abraham Doiley, citizen and slop-seller—In a word, the father consults me, the daughter complains to me, and the cousin, fille-de-chambre, romps with me. Can my importance be increased?

GRANGER [Impatiently.]
My dear Sandford!

SANDFORD
My dear Granger! The sum total is this: Old Doiley, bred, you know, in a charity school, swears he'll have a man of Larning for his son. His caprice makes him regardless of fortune; but Elizabeth's husband must have Latin at his fingers ends, and be able to teach his grandsons to sputter in Greek.

GRANGER
Oh! I'll study Hebrew, and write odes in Chaldee, if that will content him: but, may I perish, if all the pedants in England, with the Universities to back 'em, shall rob me of my Elizabeth!—See here—

[Producing a Letter.

—an invitation from her own dear hand—This morning—this very hour—in a moment I shall be at her feet—

[Going.

—Go with me through the Park—Oh, no—I cry you mercy—You walk, but I fly.

[Exit.

SANDFORD
Propitious be your flight!—Egad! there are two fine girls—I'll try 'em—half afraid—the women dress so equivocally, that one is in danger of attacking a countess, when one only means to address a nymph of King's place.

[Exit.

SCENE II.—An Apartment at Mr Doiley's

MR and **MISS DOILEY** at Breakfast.

DOILEY
Here, take away—take away. Remember, we are not at home to nobody, but to Mr Gradus.

SERVANT
The formal gentleman that was here last night, sir?

DOILEY
Yes, [snappishly] the gentleman that was here last night.

[Exit **SERVANT**.

What! I see you are resolved for to have poor Gradus's heart, Elizabeth!—I never saw you so tricked out in a morning before. But he isn't none of your chaps that's to be caught with a mountain head, nor knots, nor gewgaws—No, no; you must mind your P's and Q's with him, I can tell you. And don't laugh now when he's with you—You've a confounded knack at laughing; and there's nothing so odious in the eyes of a wise man, as a great laugher.

MISS DOILEY

Oh! his idea is as reviving as burnt feathers in hysterics.—I wish I had seen him last night, with all the rust of Oxford about him; he must have been the greatest provocative to mirth.

DOILEY

How! What! a provocative to mirth!—Why, hussey, he was recommended to me by an antikary doctor of the Royal Society—he has finished his Larning some time; and they want him to come and drink and hunt in Shropshire—Not he—he sticks to Al Mater; and the College-heads have been laid together many a time to know whether he shall be a great judge, a learned physician, or a civility doctor.

MISS DOILEY

Nay then, sir, if he's all this—laughing will be irresistible.

DOILEY

Don't put me in a passion, Betty—don't go for to put me in a passion. What, would you have a man with an eternal grin upon his face, like the head of a knocker? And hopping and skipping about like a Dutch doll with quicksilver in its heels? If you must have a husband of that sort, so be it—so be it—you know the rest.

MISS DOILEY

Surely, sir, 'tis possible for a man who does not move as if cut in wood, or speak as though he delivered his words by tail, to have breeding, and to—

DOILEY

May be—may be; but your man of breeding is not fit for old Doiley's son. What! shall I go for to give the labour of thirty years to a young jackanapes, who'll come into the room with a dancing-school step, and prate of his grandfather Sir Thomas, his great grandfather the general, and his great-great-great-grandfather, merely because I can't tell whether I ever had one or no?

MISS DOILEY

I hope, sir, that such a man could never engage my—

DOILEY

Pshaw! pshaw! you can't pretend for to judge of a man—all hypocrites and deceivers.

MISS DOILEY

Except Mr Gradus.

DOILEY

Oh, he! he's very different from your men of breeding, I assure you—The most extraordinary youth that was ever turned out of college. None of your randans, up all night—not drinking and wenching—No—in his room—poring, and reading, and studying. Oh, the joy that I shall have in hearing him talk! I do love Larning. I was grieved—grieved to the soul, Betty, when thou wert born. I had set my heart upon a boy; and if thou hadst been a boy, thou shouldst have had Greek, and algebra, and jometry enough for an archbishop.

MISS DOILEY

I am sorry—

DOILEY

No, no; don't be sorry; be obedient, and all will be as it should be. You know, I doat on you, you young slut. I left Eastcheap for Westminster, on purpose to please you.—Hav'nt I carried you to Bath, Brimmigem, and Warley-Common, and all the genteel places? I never grudge you no expence, nor no pleasure whatsomever.

MISS DOILEY

Indeed, sir, you are most indulgent.

DOILEY

Well then, don't thwart me, Betty—don't go for to thwart me, that's all. Since you came into the world, and disappointed your father of a son, 'tis your duty to give him a wise son-in-law, to make up his loss.

[Enter **CHARLOTTE**.

CHARLOTTE

Mrs Taffety, the mantua-maker, is in your dressing-room, ma'am.

DOILEY

Then send her away—she hasn't no time now for Mrs Taffety.

MISS DOILEY

Aye, send her away, Charlotte—What does she want? I didn't send for her.

CHARLOTTE

Bless me—'tis the captain. [Apart.]

MISS DOILEY

Oh, heavens! [Aside.] Yes, I do remember—Aye, I did—I did send for her about the painted lutestring.

DOILEY

Bid her come again to-morrow, I say.

CHARLOTTE

Lord bless me, sir; I dare say she can't come again to-morrow. Such mantua-makers as Mrs Taffety won't wait half a dozen times on people—Why, sir, she comes to her customers in a chair of her own; and her footman beats a tattoo at the door as if she was a countess.

DOILEY

A mantua-maker with her footman and chair! O lud! O lud! I should as soon have expected a duchess in a wheelbarrow.

MISS DOILEY

Pray, sir, allow me just to step and speak to her—It is the sweetest gown—and I'd give the world were you as much charmed with it as I am.

DOILEY

Coaxing slut!

[Exeunt **MISS DOILEY** and **CHARLOTTE**.

—Where the devil can Gradus be now?—Well, good fortune never comes in a hurry.—If I'd pitched upon your man of breeding, he'd have been here an hour ago—sipped his jocklate, kissed Elizabeth's fingers, hopped into his carriage, and away to his wench, to divert her with charatures of the old fellow and his daughter. Oh! before I'd give my gains to one of these puppies, I'd spend them all in building hospitals for lazy lacquies and decayed pimps.

[Exit.

SCENE III.—A Dressing Room

MISS DOILEY and **GRANGER**.

MISS DOILEY
A truce to your transports! Perhaps I am too much inclined to believe all you can swear—but this must be a moment of business. To secure me to yourself, are you willing to enter into measures that—

GRANGER
Any thing!—every thing! I'll have a chaise at the Park-gate in five minutes; and we'll be in Scotland, my Elizabeth, before your new lover has settled his address.

MISS DOILEY
Pho! pho! you're a mere bungler at contrivance; if you'll be guided by me, my father shall give me to you at St James's Church, in the face of the world.

GRANGER
Indeed!

MISS DOILEY
Indeed.

GRANGER
I fear to trust to it, my angel! Beauty can work miracles with all mankind; but an obstinate father—

MISS DOILEY
It is you who must work the miracle. I have settled the whole affair with my cousin, who has understanding and wit—and you have only to be obedient.

GRANGER
I am perfectly obedient—Pray, give me my lesson.

MISS DOILEY
Why, luckily, you know my father has never seen you—he left Bath before you had the sauciness—

[Enter **CHARLOTTE** with a Bundle.

CHARLOTTE
There! you're finely caught!—Here's your father and Mr Gradus actually upon the stairs, coming here.

GRANGER
Zounds! where's the closet?

MISS DOILEY
Oh, Lord! here's no closet—I shall faint with terror.

GRANGER
No back stairs? No clothes press?

CHARLOTTE
Neither, neither! But here—I'm your guardian angel—

[Untying the Bundle

—I told 'em Mrs Taffety was here; so, without more ceremony, clap on these—speak broken English, and my life for it, you'll pass muster with my uncle.

GRANGER
What! make a woman of me? By Jupiter—

CHARLOTTE
Lay your commands on him—If he doesn't submit, we are ruined.

MISS DOILEY
Oh, you shall, I protest. Here, I'll put his cap on.

DOILEY [Without.]
This way, sir—come this way—We'll take her by surprise—least preparation is best.

[Pulling at the Door.

Open the door!

MISS DOILEY
Presently, sir.

DOILEY [Knocking.]
What the dickens are you doing, I say? Open the door!

CHARLOTTE
In a moment—I'm only pinning my cousin's gown—Lord bless me! you hurry one so, you have made me prick my finger.—There, now you may enter.

[Enter **DOILEY** and **GRADUS**.

DOILEY
Oh! only my daughter's mantua-maker.—

[**GRANGER** makes curtseys, and goes out followed by **CHARLOTTE**.

Here Elizabeth, this is that Mr Gradus I talked to you about. Bless me! I hope you a'n't ill—you look as white as a candle.

MISS DOILEY
No, sir, not ill; but this woman has fretted me to death—she has spoiled my gown.

DOILEY
Why then, make her pay for it, d'ye hear? It's my belief, if she was to pay for all she spoils, she'd soon drop her chair, and trudge a foot. Mr Gradus—beg pardon—this is my daughter—don't think the worse of her because she's a little dash'd, or so.

GRADUS
Bashfulness, Mr Doiley, is the robe of modesty—and modesty, as hath been well observed, is a sunbeam of a diamond—giving force to its beauty, and exalting its lustre.

DOILEY
He was a deep one, I warrant him, that said that—I remember something like it in the Wisdom of Solomon. Come, speak to Elizabeth there—I see she won't till you've broke the ice.

GRADUS
Madam!—

[Bows.

—hem—permit me—this honour—hem—believe me, lady, I have more satisfaction in beholding you, than I should have in conversing with Grævius and Gronovius; I had rather possess your approbation than that of the elder Scaliger; and this apartment is more precious to me than was the Lyceum Portico to the most zealous of the Peripatetics.

DOILEY [Aside.]
There! Shew me a man of breeding who could talk so!

MISS DOILEY
I believe all you have said to be very fine, sir; but unfortunately, I don't know the gentlemen you mentioned. The education given to women shuts us entirely from such refined acquaintance.

GRADUS
Perfectly right, madam, perfectly right. The more simple your education, the nearer you approach the pure manners of the purest ages. The charms of women were never more powerful—never inspired such achievements, as in those immortal periods, when they could neither read nor write.

DOILEY

Not read nor write! zounds, what a time was that for to bring up a daughter! Why, a peeress in those days did not cost so much as a barber's daughter in ours. Miss Friz must have her dancing, her French, her tambour, her harpsicholl, her jography, her stronomy—whilst her father, to support all this, lives upon sprats: or, once in two years, calls his creditors to a composition.

GRADUS

Oh, tempora mutantur! but these exuberances, Mr Doiley, indigitate unbounded liberty.

DOILEY

Digitate or not—ifackens, if the ladies would take my advice, they'd return to their distaffs, and grow notable—to distinguish themselves from their shopkeepers' wives.

GRADUS

Ah! it was at the loom, and the spinning wheel, that the Lucretias and Portias of the world imbibed their virtue; that the mothers of the Gracchi, the Horatii, the Antonini, caught that sacred flame with which they inspired their sons, and with the milk of their own pure bosoms gave them that fortitude, that magnanimity, which made them conquerors, kings.

[Enter a **SERVANT**.

SERVANT

Sir, here's a Lord! Lord Pharo!

DOILEY

Lord Pharo! hum, then the four aces run against him last night. Well, the ill-luck of some, and the fine taste of others, makes my money breed like rabbits. [Aside.]

SERVANT

Sir—

DOILEY

Well, well, I'm coming—When a lord wants money, he'll wait as patiently as any body. Well, Mr Gradus, I'm your humble sarvant. Elizabeth!—you understand me.

[Exit.

GRADUS

How unlucky the old gentleman should be called away! Hem! [Addressing himself to speak to her.] There is something in her eyes so sarcastic, I'd rather pronounce the Terræ-filius, than address her. Madam!—What can I say? Oh, now—that's fortunate.

[Pulling out some Papers.

Hem! I will venture to request your ideas, madam, on a little autographon, which I design for the world.

MISS DOILEY

Sir!

GRADUS

In which I have, found a new chronometer, to prove that Confucius and Zoroaster were the same person;—and that the Pyramids are not so ancient, by two hundred years, as the world believes.

MISS DOILEY

To what purpose, sir?

GRADUS

Purpose!—Purpose, madam! Why, really, Miss, our booksellers' shelves are loaded with volumes in the unfruitful road of plain sense and nature, and unless an author can elance himself from the common track, he stands as little chance to be known, as a comet in its aphelion. Pray, ma'am, amuse yourself.

MISS DOILEY

O Lord, sir! you may as well offer me a sheet of hieroglyphics—besides, I hate reading.

GRADUS

Hate reading!

MISS DOILEY

Ay, to be sure; what's reading good for, but to give a stiff embarrassed air? It makes a man move as if made by a carpenter, who had forgot to give him joints—[Observing him.] He twirls his hat, and bites his thumb, whilst his hearers, his beholders, I mean, are gaping for his wit.

GRADUS

The malicious creature! 'tis my picture she has been drawing, and now 'tis more impossible for me to speak than ever.

MISS DOILEY

For my part—for my part, if I was a man, I'd study only dancing and bonmots. With no other learning than these, he may be light and frolicksome as Lady Airy's ponies; but loaded with Greek, philosophy, and mathematics, he's as heavy and dull as a cart horse.

GRADUS

Fæmina cum voce diaboli.

MISS DOILEY

Bless me, sir! why are you silent? My father told me you was a lover—I never saw such a lover in my life. By this time you should have said fifty brilliant things—found an hundred similes for my eyes, complexion, and wit. Can your memory furnish you with nothing pat?—No poetry—no heroics! What subject did Portia's lovers entertain her with, while she sat spinning—aye?

GRADUS

The lovers of that age, madam, were ignorant of frothy compliments. Instead of being gallant, they were brave; instead of flattery, they studied virtue and wisdom. It was these, madam, that nerved the Roman arm; that empowered her to drag the nations of the world at her chariot wheels, and that raised to such an exalted height—

MISS DOILEY

That down she tumbled in the dust—and there I beg you'll leave her. Was ever any thing so monstrous! I ask for a compliment and you begin an oration—an oration on a parcel of stiff warriors, and formal pedants. Why, sir, there is not one of these brave, wise, godlike men, but will appear as ridiculous in a modern assembly as a judge in his long wig and a maccaroni jacket.

GRADUS

Now I am dumb again. Oh, that I had you at Brazen-nose, madam!—I could manage you there. [Aside.]

MISS DOILEY

What! now you're in the pouts, sir? 'Tis mighty well. Bless us! what a life a wife must lead with such a being! for ever talking sentences, or else in profound silence. No delightful nonsense, no sweet trifling. All must be solemn, wise, and grave. Hang me if I would not sooner marry the bust of Seneca, in bronze—then I should have all the gravity and coldness of wisdom, without its impertinence.

GRADUS

The impertinence of wisdom!—Surely, madam, or I am much deceived, you possess a mind capable of—

MISS DOILEY

Now I see, by the twist of your chin, sir, you are beginning another oration—but, I protest, I will never hear you speak again, till you have forsworn those tones, and that manner. Go, sir,—throw your books into the fire, turn your study into a dressing-room, hire a dancing-master, and grow agreeable.

[Exit.

GRADUS

Plato! Aristotle! Zeno! I abjure ye. A girl bred in a nursery, in whose soul the sacred lamp of knowledge hath scarcely shed its faintest rays, hath vanquished, and struck dumb, the most faithful of your disciples.

[Enter **CHARLOTTE**.

Here's another she-devil, I'd as soon encounter a she-wolf.

[Going.

CHARLOTTE

Stay, sir, pray, an instant! Lord bless me! am I such a scare-crow? I was never run from by a young man before in my life.

[Pulls him back.

GRADUS

I resolve henceforward to run from your whole sex—Youth and beauty are only other names for coquetry and affectation. Let me go, madam, you have beauty, and doubtless all that belongs to it.

CHARLOTTE

Lud! you've a mighty pretty whimsical way of complimenting—Miss Doiley might have discerned something in you worth cherishing, in spite of that husk of scholarship. To pass one's life with such a being, seems to me to be the very apex of human felicity.—I found that word for him in a book of geometry this morning. [Aside.]

GRADUS
Indeed!

CHARLOTTE
Positively. I have listen'd to your conversation, and I can't help being concerned that talents which ought to do you honour, should, by your mismanagement, be converted into downright ridicule.

GRADUS
This creature is of a genus quite different from the other. She has understanding! [Aside.]—I begin to suspect, madam, that though I have some knowledge, I have still much to learn.

CHARLOTTE
You have indeed—knowledge; as you manage it, it is a downright bore.

GRADUS
Boar! What relation can there be between knowledge and a hog!

CHARLOTTE
Lord bless me! how ridiculous! You have spent your life in learning the dead languages, and ignorant of the living—Why, sir, bore is all the ton.

GRADUS
Ton! ton! What may that be? It cannot be orthology: I do not recollect its root in the parent languages.

CHARLOTTE
Ha! ha! ha! better and better. Why, sir, ton means—ton is—Pho! what signifies where the root is? These kinds of words are the short hand of conversation, and convey whole sentences at once. All one likes is ton, and all one hates is bore.

GRADUS
And is that divine medium, which pourtrays our minds, and makes us first in the animal climax! is speech become so arbitrary, that—

CHARLOTTE
Divine medium! animal climax! [Contemptuously.] You know very well, the use of language is to express one's likes and dislikes—and a pig will do this as effectually by its squeak, or a hen with her cackle, as you with your Latin and Greek.

GRADUS
What can I say to you?

CHARLOTTE
Nothing;—but yield yourself to my guidance, and you shall conquer Miss Doiley.

GRADUS

Conquer her! she's so incased with ridicule, there is not a single vulnerable spot about her.

CHARLOTTE

Pshaw, pshaw! What becomes of her ridicule, when you have banish'd your absurdities! One can no more exist without the other, than the mundane system without air. There's a touch of my science for you. [Aside.]

GRADUS

Madam, I'll take you for my Minerva—Cover me with your shield, and lead me to battle.

CHARLOTTE

Enough. In the first place,

[Leading him to a Glass.

—in the first place, don't you think you are habited a la mode d'amour? Did you ever see a Cupid in a grizzle wig, curled as stifly as Sir Cloudsley Shovel's in the Abbey? A dingy brown coat, with vellum button holes, to be sure, speaks an excellent taste: but then I would advise you to lay it by in lavender, for your grandson's christening—and here's cambric enough in your ruffles to make his shirt.

GRADUS

I perceive my error. The votaries of love commence a new childhood; and dignity would be as unbecoming in them, as a hornpipe to a Socrates—But habit is so strong, that, to gain an empress, I could not assume that careless air, that promptness of expression—

CHARLOTTE

Then you may give up the pursuit of Miss Doiley—for such a wise piece of uprightness would stand as good a chance to be secretary to the coterie, as her husband.

GRADUS

It is Mr Doiley, who will—

CHARLOTTE

Mr Doiley! ridiculous—Depend on't he'll let her marry just whom she will—This Mr Gradus, says he— why, I don't care a groat whether you marry him or no, says he—there are fifty young fellows at Oxford who can talk Greek as well as he—

GRADUS

Indeed?

CHARLOTTE

I have heard a good account of the young man, says he. But all I ask of you is, to receive two visits from him—no more than two visits. If you don't like him—so; if you do, I'll give you half my fortune on the day of marriage, and the rest at my death.

GRADUS

What a singularity! to limit me to two visits—One is already past, and she hates me—What can I expect from the other?

CHARLOTTE
Every thing. It is a moment that decides the fate of a lover. Now fancy me Miss Doiley—swear I'm a divinity—then take my hand, and press it—thus.

GRADUS
Heavens! her touch has thrill'd me.

CHARLOTTE
And if I should pout and resent the liberty, make your apology on my lips.

[**GRADUS** catches her in his Arms, and kisses her.

So, so, you have fire, I perceive.

GRADUS
Can you give me any more lessons?

CHARLOTTE
Yes; but this is not the place. I have a friend—Mr Sandford, whom you saw here last night—you shall dine with him: he will initiate you at once in the fashionable rage, and teach you to trifle agreeably. You shall be equipp'd from his wardrobe, to appear here in the evening a man of the world—Adieu to Grizzles, and—

GRADUS
But what will the father think of such a metamorphosis?

CHARLOTTE
Study your mistress only—your visit will be to her, and that visit decides your fate. Resolve then to take up your new character boldly—in all its strongest lines, or give up one of the richest heiresses in the kingdom.

GRADUS
My obligations, madam—

CHARLOTTE
Don't stay, now, to run the risk of meeting Mr Doiley—for, if he should discover that you have disgusted his daughter, Sandford, the dinner, and the plot, will be worth no more than your gravity. Away, I'll meet you at Story's Gate to introduce you.

[Exit **GRADUS**.

[Enter **MISS DOILEY**.

MISS DOILEY
Excellent Charlotte! you've outgone my expectation—did ever a woodcock run so blindly into a snare?

CHARLOTTE

Oh, that's the way of all your great scholars—take them but an inch out of their road, and you may turn 'em inside out, as easily as your glove.

MISS DOILEY

Well, but have you seen Sandford?—Is every thing in train?—Will Gradus be hoodwink'd?

CHARLOTTE

Hoodwink'd! Why, don't you see he's already stark blind? or, if he has any eyes, I assure ye they are all for me.

MISS DOILEY

My heart palpitates with apprehension—We shall never succeed.

CHARLOTTE

Oh, I'll answer for the scholar, if you'll undertake the soldier. Mr Sandford has engaged half a dozen of the Scavoir vivre; all in high spirits at the idea of tricking old Leatherpurse—and they have sworn to exhaust wit and invention, to turn our Solon out of their hands a finished coxcomb.

MISS DOILEY

Blessing on their labours! My Granger is gone to study his rival; and will make I hope a tolerable copy. Now follow Gradus, my dear Charlotte, and take care they give him just champagne enough to raise him to the point, without turning over it.

[Exeunt.

ACT II

SCENE I.—An Apartment

DOILEY asleep. A Table before him, with Bottles, &c. &c.

[Enter a **SERVANT**.

Serv. Sir! Sir!

[Jogging him.

Sir! What a pise! sure my master has drain'd the bottles, he sleeps so sound—Oh, no—

[Pours out a Glass.

—Here's t'ye, old gentleman! can't think why they send me to wake thee—am sure the house is always quietest when you're a snoring.—

[Drinks, then awakens him.

DOILEY
Hey!—how I—what! Is Mr Gradus come?

Serv. No, sir—but Mr Sandford's above stairs, and a mortal fine gentleman.

DOILEY
Fine gentleman!—aye—some rake, I suppose, that wants to sell an annuity—I wonder where Gradus is—past seven

[Looking at his Watch.

SERVANT
His friends keep the gentleman over a bottle, mayhap, sir, longer than he thought for.

DOILEY
He over a bottle?—more liker he's over some crabbed book—or watching what the moon's about, through a microscope. Come move the things; and empty them two bottoms into one bottle, and cork it up close—d'ye hear—I wish Gradus was come—Well, if I succeed in this one point, the devil may run away with the rest. Let the world go to loggerheads; grass grow upon 'Change: land-tax mount up; little Doiley is snug. Doiley, with a hundred thousand in annuities, and a son-in-law as wise as a chancellor, may bid defiance to wind and weather.

[Exit.

SCENE II.—A Drawing Room

Enter **GRADUS**, led by **CHARLOTTE**, and followed by **MR SANDFORD**.

CHARLOTTE
Well, I protest this is an improvement!—Why, what with sattins and tassels, and spangles and foils, you look as fine as a chymist's shop by candle-light.

GRADUS
Madam do you approve—

CHARLOTTE
Oh, amazingly—I'll run and send Miss Doiley to admire you.

GRADUS [Looking in a Glass.]
Oh, if our proctor could now behold me! he would never believe that figure to be Jeremy Gradus.

SANDFORD
Very true, and I give ye joy. No one would conceive you'd ever been within gun-shot of a college.

GRADUS

What must I do with this?

SANDFORD

Your chapeau bras—wear it thus. These hats are for the arm only.

GRADUS

A hat for the arm! what a subversion of ideas; Oh, Mr Sandford—if the sumptuary laws of Lycurgus—

SANDFORD

Damn it! will you never leave off your college cant? I tell you once more—and, by Jupiter, if you don't attend to me, I'll give you up—I say, you must forget that such fellows ever existed—that there was ever a language but English—a classic but Ovid, or a volume but his Art of Love.

GRADUS

I will endeavour to form myself from your instructions—but tarry with me, I entreat you—if you should leave me—

SANDFORD

I won't leave you. Here's your mistress—Now, Gradus, stand to your arms.

GRADUS

I'll do my best—but I could wish the purse-keeper was Miss Charlotte.

[Enter **MISS DOILEY**.

SANDFORD

Hush! Your devoted: allow me, madam, to introduce a gentleman to you, in whose affairs I am particularly interested—Mr Gradus.

MISS DOILEY

Mr Gradus! Is it possible?

GRADUS

Be not astonished, Oh lovely maiden, at my sudden change! Beauty is a talisman which works true miracles, and, without a fable, transforms mankind.

MISS DOILEY

Your transformation, I fear, is too sudden to be lasting—

GRADUS

Transformation! Resplendent Virgo! brightest constellation of the starry sone! I am but now created. Your charms, like the Promethean fire, have warm'd the clod to life, and rapt me to a new existence.

MISS DOILEY

But may I be sure you'll never take up your old rust again?

GRADUS

Never. Sooner shall Taurus with the Pisces join, Copernicus to Ptolemy resign the spheres, than I be what I was.

MISS DOILEY [Aside.]
I shall burst.

SANDFORD
Well, you've hit it off tolerably, for a coup d'essai—But prythee, Gradus, can't you talk in a style a little less fustian? You remember how those fine fellows conversed you saw at dinner; no sentences, no cramp words—all was ease and impudence.

GRADUS
Yes, I remember. Now the shell is burst, I shall soon be fledged.

[**DOILEY** entering starts back.

DOILEY
Why, who the Dickens have we here?

SANDFORD
So, there's the old genius!

MISS DOILEY
But I am convinced now—I am convinced now this is all put on—in your heart you are still Mr Gradus.

GRADUS
Yes, madam, still Gradus; but not that stiff scholastic fool you saw this morning: No, no, I've learned that the acquisitions of which your father is so ridiculously fond, are useless lumber; that a man who knows more than his neighbours is in danger of being shut out of society: or, at best, of being invited at dinner once in a twelvemonth, to be exhibited like an antique bronze, or a porridge-pot from Herculaneum.

DOILEY
Zounds! 'tis he! I'm all over in a cold sweat. [Behind.]

MISS DOILEY
And don't you think learning the greatest blessing in the world?

GRADUS
Not I, truly, madam—Learning! a vile bore!

DOILEY
Do I stand upon my head or my heels?

GRADUS
I shall leave all those fopperies to the grey-beards at college. Let 'em chop logic, or make English hashes out of stale Hebrew, till they starve, for me.

SANDFORD

This is your resolution?

GRADUS
Fixed as Ixion on his wheel, I have no study now but the ton.

DOILEY
Indeed!

GRADUS
You shall confess, my friend, in spite of prejudice, that 'tis possible for a man of letters to become a man of the world. You shall see that he can dress, grow an adept in the science of taste, ogle at the opera, be vociferous at the playhouse, suffer himself to be pigeon'd with an easy air at Boodle's, and lose his health for the benefit of his reputation in King's Place.

MISS DOILEY
Bless me! one would suppose you had been familiar in the bon ton all your life—you have all the requisites to make a figure in it, my heart.

GRADUS
The mere force of beauty, madam—I wished to become worthy of you, and that wish has work'd a miracle.

DOILEY
A miracle with a vengeance! Jacquet Droz's wood and wire-work was nothing to it.

MISS DOILEY
How different from what you was this morning!

GRADUS
Oh, mention it not—This morning—may it be blotted from Time's ledger, and never thought on more! I abhor my former self, madam, more than you can: witness now the recantation of my errors. Learning, with all its tribe of solemn fopperies, I abjure—abjure for ever.

DOILEY
You do?

GRADUS
The study of what is vulgarly called philosophy, may suit a monk: but it is as unbecoming a gentleman, as loaded dice, or a brass-hilted sword.

DOILEY
Larning unbecoming a gentleman!—Very well!

GRADUS
Hebrew I leave to the Jew rabbies, Greek to the bench of bishops, Latin to the apothecaries, and astronomy to almanack-makers.

DOILEY

Better and better.

GRADUS
The mathematics—mixed, pure, speculative, and practical, with their whole circle of sciences, I consign in a lump to old men who want blood, and to young ones who want bread. And now you've heard my whole abjuration.

[**DOILEY** rushing forward.

DOILEY
Yes—and I have heard too—I have heard. Oh, that I should ever have been such a dolt, as to take thee for a man of larning!

GRADUS [Confounded.]
Mr Doiley!

DOILEY
What? don't be dash'd, man: go on with your abjurations, do. Yes, you'll make a shine in the tone?—Oh, that ever I should have been such a nincompoop!

SANDFORD
My dear Mr Doiley, do not be in a heat. How can a man of your discernment—Now look at Gradus—I'm sure he's a much prettier fellow than he was—his figure and his manner are quite different things.

DOILEY
Yes, yes, I can see that—I can see that—Why, he has turn'd little Easop upside down—he's the lion in the skin of an ass.

[Walking about.

GRADUS
I must retrieve myself in his opinion. The skin, Mr Doiley, may be put off; and be assured, that the mind which has once felt the sacred energies of wisdom, though it may assume, for a moment—

MISS DOILEY [Angrily.]
So, so!

SANDFORD [Apart.]
Hark ye, sir, that won't do. By heav'n, if you play retrograde, I'll forsake you on the spot. You are ruined with your mistress in a moment.

GRADUS
Dear madam! believe me, that as for—What can I say!—How assimilate myself to two such opposite tastes? I stand reeling here between two characters, like a substantive between two adjectives.

DOILEY
You! you for to turn fop and maccaroni! Why, 'twould be as natural for a Jew rabbin to turn parson. An elephant in pinners—a bishop with a rattle and bells; couldn't be more posterous.

SANDFORD
Nay, now, my dear Mr Doiley—

DOILEY
Dear me no dears. Why, if I wanted a maccaroni, I might have had choice; every alley from Hyde Park to Shadwell Dock swarms with 'em—genuine; and d'ye think I'll have an amphiberous thing—half and half, like the sea-calf at Sir Ashton's?

SANDFORD
Oh, if that's all, an hundred to ten, Gradus will soon be as complete a character, as if he had never learnt his alpha beta: or known more of the classics than their names.

DOILEY
Oh, I warrant him. Now, what do ye think of the Scratchi, the Horsi, and the rest of 'em? aye?

GRADUS
Oh, a mere bore! a parcel of brawny untaught fellows, who knew no more of life than they did of Chinese. If they'd stood candidates for rank in a college of taste, they'd have been returned ignorantur—Would they not, madam?

MISS DOILEY
Oh, certainly.—I could kiss the fellow, he has entered into my plot with such spirit.

[Exit.

DOILEY
Why, you've been in wonderful haste to get rid of the igranter part—but as it happened, that was the only part I cared for; so now you may carry your hogs to another market; they won't do for me.

GRADUS
My hogs!

DOILEY
Aye, your boars—your improvements—your fashionable airs—your—in short, you are not the man I took you for; so you may trot back to college again; go, mister, and teach 'em the tone, do. Lord, how they'll stare! Jeremy Gradus, or the monkey returned from travel!

SANDFORD
Upon my honour, you are too severe. Leave us, man—leave us—I'll settle your affair, I warrant. [To **GRADUS**.]

GRADUS
Not so easily, I fear—he sticks to his point like a rusty weather-cock—All my dependance is on the lady.

SANDFORD
You'll allow Gradus to speak to Miss Doiley?

DOILEY

Oh, aye, to be sure—the more he speaks the less she'll like him. Here, shew Mr Gradus the dressing-room.

[Exit **GRADUS**.]

Give her another dose; surfeit her by all means.—Why, sure, Mr Sandford, you had no hand in transmogrifying the—

SANDFORD

Yes, faith I had. I couldn't endure the idea of seeing your charming daughter tied to a collection of Greek apothegms, and Latin quotations; so I endeavoured to English him.

DOILEY

English him! I take it shocking ill of you, Mr Sandford—that I must tell you—Here are all my hopes gone like a whiff of tobacco!

SANDFORD

Pho! my dear Mr Doiley, this attachment of yours to scholarship is a mere whim—

DOILEY

Whim!—Well, suppose it is, I will have my whim. Worked hard forty years, and saved above twice as many thousand pounds; and if so much labour, and so much money, won't entitle a man to whim, I don't know what the devil should.

SANDFORD

Nor I either, I'm sure.

DOILEY

To tell you a bit of a secret—lack of larning has been my great detriment. If I'd been a scholar, there's no knowing what I mought have got—my plumb might have been two—my—

SANDFORD

Why, doubtless a little classical knowledge might have been useful in driving your bargains for Russia tallow, and whale blubber.

DOILEY

Aye, to be sure! And I do verily believe it hindered me from being Lord Mayor—only think of that—Lord Mayor of London!

SANDFORD

How so?

DOILEY

Why I tended the common council and all the parish meetings for fifteen years, without daring for to make one arangue; at last a westry was called about chusing of a turncock. So now, thinks I, I'll shew 'em what I'm good for.—Our alderman was in the purples—so, thinks I, if he tips off, why not I as well as another?—So I'll make a speech about patrots, and then ax for their votes.

SANDFORD
Very judicious!

DOILEY
If you'll believe me, I got up three times—Silence! says Mr Cryer; and my tongue grew so dry with fright, that I couldn't wag it; so I was forced to squat down again, 'midst horse-laughs; and they nick-named me Dummy, through the whole ward.

SANDFORD
Wicked rogues! Well, I ask your pardon—I had no idea of these important reasons. Yet, how men differ! Now the family of Sir Wilford Granger are quite distressed by the obstinate attachment to the sciences of that fine young fellow I told you of this morning.

DOILEY
Aye! What's he Sir Wilford Granger's son? Knew his father very well—kept a fine study of horses, and lost many thousands by it; lent him money many a time—good man—always punctual.

SANDFORD
Aye, sir, but this youth disappointed all his hopes. Mighty pleasant, to see a young fellow, formed to possess life in all its points and bewitching varieties, shrink from the world, and bury himself amidst obsolete books, systems, and schisms, whilst pleasure wooes him to her soft embrace, and joy solicits him in vain! Oh, it gave his father great trouble.

DOILEY
Great trouble! Dear me, dear me! I always thought Sir Wilford had been a wiser man—Why, I would have given the world for such a son.

SANDFORD
He swallows it rarely! [Aside.]—Oh, he piques himself on such trifles as reading the Greek and Latin authors in their own tongues, and mastering all the quibbles of our English philosophers—

DOILEY
English philosophers! I wouldn't give a farthing for them.

SANDFORD
Why, sure you have heard of a Bacon, a Locke, a Newton—

DOILEY
Newton! oh, aye—I have heard of Sir Isaac—every body has heard of Sir Isaac—great man—Master of the Mint.

SANDFORD
Oh, sir! this youth has found a dozen mistakes in his theories, and proved him wrong in one or two of his calculations. In short, he is advised to give the world a system of his own, in which, for aught I know, he'll prove the earth to be concave instead of spherical, and the moon to be no bigger than a punch-bowel.

DOILEY [Aside.]
He's the man—he's the man!—Look'e, Mr Sandford, you've given a description of this young fellow, that's set my blood in a ferment. Do you—now, my dear friend, do you think now that you could prevail upon him to marry my daughter?

SANDFORD
Why, I don't know—neither beauty nor gold has charms for him. Knowledge—knowledge is his mistress.

DOILEY
Aye! I'm sorry for that—and yet I'm glad of it too. Now, see what ye can do with him—see what ye can do with him!

SANDFORD
Well, well, I'll try. He promised to call on me here this evening, in his way to the Museum. I don't know whether he isn't below now.

DOILEY
Below now! Ifackins, that's lucky—hang me if it isn't! Do, go and—and speak to him a bit—and bring him up—bring him up. Tell him, if he'll marry Elizabeth, I'll give him, that is, I'll leave him every farthing I have in the world.

SANDFORD
Well, since you are so very earnest, I'll see what I can do.

[Exit.

DOILEY
Thank'e, thank'e! I'cod! I'll buy him twice as many books as a college library, but what I'll bribe him—that I will. What the dickens can Elizabeth be about with that thing there, that Gradus! He a man of larning! Hang me if I don't believe his head's as hallow as my cane. Shure she can't have taken a fancy to the smattering monkey! Ho, there they are—here he comes! Why there's Greek and Algebra in his face.

[Enter **SANDFORD** and **GRANGER** dressed in black.

Mr Granger, your very humble sarvant, sir,—I'm very glad to see you, sir.

GRANGER [Very solemnly.]
I thank you, sir.

DOILEY
I knew your father, sir, as well as a beggar knows his dish. Mayhap Mr Sandford told you that I wanted for to bring you and my daughter acquainted—I'll go and call her in.

GRANGER
'Tis unnecessary.

DOILEY [Apart.]
He seems a mighty silent man.

SANDFORD

Studying—studying. Ten to one he's forming a discourse Arabic, or revolving one of Euclid's problems.

DOILEY

Couldn't you set him a talking a bit? I long for to hear him talk.

SANDFORD

Come, man! forget the old sages a moment. Can't the idea of Miss Doiley give a fillip to your imagination?

GRANGER

Miss Doiley, I'm informed, is as lovely as a woman can be. But what is woman?—Only one of Nature's agreeable blunders.

DOILEY

Hum! That smacks of something! [Aside.] Why, as to that, Mr Granger, a woman with no portion but her whims, might be but a kind of a Jew's bargain; but when fifty thousand is popt into the scale, she must be bad indeed, if her husband does not find her a pen'worth.

GRANGER

With men of the world, Mr Doiley, fifty thousand pounds might have their weight; but, in the balance of philosophy, gold is light as dephlogisticated air.

DOILEY

That's deep—I can make nothing of it—that must be deep. [Aside.] Mr Granger! the great account I have heard of your larning, and whatnot, has made me willing for to be a kin to you.

GRANGER

Mr Sandford suggested to me your design, sir; and as you have so nobly proposed your daughter as the prize of learning, I have an ambition to be related to you.

DOILEY [Aside.]

But I'll see a bit farther into him though, first. Now pray, Mr Granger! pray now—a—I say [To **SANDFORD**.] Ax him some deep question, that he may shew himself a bit.

SANDFORD

What the devil shall I say? A deep question you would have it? Let me see!—Oh, Granger, is it your opinion that the ancient antipodes walked erect, or crawled on all four?

GRANGER

A thinking man always doubts—but the best informations concur, that they were quadrupedes during two revolutions of the sun, and bipedes ever after.

DOILEY [Aside.]

Quadpedes! Bipedes! What a fine man he is!

SANDFORD

A surprising transformation!

GRANGER
Not more surprising than the transformation of an eruca to a chrysalis, a chrysalis to a nymph, and a nymph to a butterfly.

DOILEY
There again! I see it will do—I see it will do—aye, that I will—hang me if I don't. [Aside.]

[Exit, chuckling and laughing.

GRANGER
What's he gone off for, so abruptly?

SANDFORD
For his daughter, I hope. Give ye joy, my dear fellow! the nymph, the eruca, and the chrysalis have won the day.

GRANGER
How shall I bound my happiness? My dear Sandford, that was the luckiest question, about the antipodes.

SANDFORD
Yes, pretty successful. Have you been at your studies?

GRANGER
Oh, I've been in the Dictionary this half hour; and have picked up cramp words enough to puzzle and delight the old gentleman the remainder of his life.

SANDFORD
Here he is, faith—

GRANGER
And Elizabeth with him—I hear her dear footsteps! Oh, how shall I—

DOILEY [Without]
Come along, I say—what a plague are you so modest for? Come in here,

[Pulls in **GRADUS** by the Arm]

Here, I've brought him—one of your own kidney—ha! ha! ha! Now I'll lay you a gallon you can't guess what I've brought him for; I've brought him—ha! ha! ha! for to pit him against you [to **GRANGER**] to see which of you two is the most larned—ha! ha!

GRANGER
Ten thousand devils, plagues, and furies!

SANDFORD

Here's a blow up!

DOILEY
Why, for all he looks so like a nincompoop in this pye-pick'd jacket, he's got his noddle full of Greek and Algebra, and them things. Why, Gradus, don't stand aloof, man—this is a brother scholar, I tell ye.

GRADUS
A scholar! all who have earn'd that distinction are my brethren. Carissme frater, gaudeo te videre.

GRANGER
Sir—you—I—most obedient. I wish thou wert in the bottom of the Red Sea, and the largest folio in thy library about thy neck. [Aside.]

SANDFORD
For heaven's sake, Mr Doiley, what do you mean?

DOILEY
Mean! why I mean for to pit 'em, to be sure, and to give Elizabeth to the winner.—Touch him up, touch him up! [To **GRANGER**.] Shew him what a fool he is.

SANDFORD
Why, sure you won't set them together by the ears!

DOILEY
No, no; but I'm resolved to set them together by the tongues. To cut the business short—Mr Gradus! you are to be sure a great dab at larning, and what not; but I'll bet my daughter, and fifty thousand to boot, that Granger beats ye—and he that wins shall have her.

GRANGER
Heavens, what a stake! 'Tis sufficient to inspire a dolt with the tongues of Babel.

SANDFORD
My dear friend, think of the indelicacy—

DOILEY
Fiddle-de-dee!—I tell you, I will have my whim—and so, Gradus, set off. By Jenkin! you'll find it a tough business to beat Granger—he's one of your great genis men—going to write a book about Sir Isaac, and the Moon, and the devil knows what.

[**MISS DOILEY** and **CHARLOTTE** enter at the back of the Stage.

GRADUS
If so, the more glorious will be my victory. Come, sir, let us enter the lists, since it must be so, for this charming prize.

[Pointing to **MISS DOILEY**.

Chuse your weapons—Hebrew—Greek—Latin, or English. Name your subject; we will pursue it syllogistically, or socratically, as you please.

GRANGER [Aside.]
Curse your syllogisms, and Socraticisms!

DOILEY
No, no; I'll not have no English—What a plague! every shoe-black jabbers English—so give us a touch of Greek to set off with. Come, Gradus, you begin.

MISS DOILEY
Undone! undone!

GRADUS
If it is merely a recitation of Greek that you want, you shall be gratified. An epigram that occurs to me, will give you an idea of that sublime language.

CHARLOTTE [Aside.]
Oh, confound your sublime language!

GRADUS
Panta gelos, kai panta konis kai panta to meden
Panta gar exalagon, esti taginomena.

DOILEY
Panta tri pantry? Why, that's all about the pantry. What, the old Grecians loved tit-bits, mayhap; but that's low! ay, Sandford!

SANDFORD
Oh, cursed low! he might as well have talked about a pig-stye.

DOILEY
Come, Granger, now for it! Elizabeth and fifty thousand pounds!

GRANGER
Yes, sir. I—I—am not much prepared; I could wish—I could wish—Sandford! [Apart.]

SANDFORD
Zounds! say something—any thing!

CHARLOTTE [Aside.]
Eigh! it's all over. He could as easily furnish the ways and means, as a word in Greek.

DOILEY
Hoity, toity! What, at a stand! Why, sure you can talk Greek as well as Gradus.

GRANGER

'Tis a point I cannot decide; you must determine it. Now, impudence, embrace me with thy seven-fold shield! Zanthus, I remember, in describing such a night as this—

GRADUS
Zanthus! you surely err. Homer mentions but one being of that name, except a river, and he was a horse.

GRANGER
Sir, he was an orator; and such an one, that Homer records, the Gods themselves inspired him.

GRADUS
True, sir; but you won't deny—

DOILEY
Come, come! I sha'n't have no browbeating; nobody offered for to contradict you; so begin. [To **GRANGER**.] What said orator Zanthus?

GRANGER
Yon lucid orb, in æther pensile, irradiates the expanse. Refulgent scintillations, in the ambient void opake, emit humid splendor. Chrysalic spheroids the horizon vivify—astifarious constellations, nocturnal sporades, in refrangerated radit, illume our orb terrene.

MISS DOILEY [Aside.]
I breathe again!

DOILEY
There, there! Well spoke, Granger! Now, Gradus, beat that!

GRADUS
I am enwrapt in astonishment! You are imposed on, sir. Instead of classical language, you have heard a rant in English—

DOILEY
English! zounds! d'ye take me for a fool? D'ye think I don't know my own mother-tongue!—'Twas no more like English, than I am like Whittington's cat.

GRADUS
It was every syllable English.

DOILEY
There's impudence! There wasn't no word of it English. If you take that for English, devil take me if I believe there was a word of Greek in all your tri-pantrys.

GRADUS
Oh! the torture of ignorance!

DOILEY

Ignorant! Come, come, none of your tricks upon travellers. I know you mean all that as a skit upon my edication; but I'd have you to know, sir, that I'll read the hardest chapter of Nehemiah with you, for your ears.

GRADUS
I repeat that you are imposed on. Mr Sandford, I appeal to you.

GRANGER
And I appeal—

SANDFORD
Nay, gentlemen, Mr Doiley is your judge in all disputes concerning the vulgar tongue.

DOILEY
Aye, to be sure I am. Who cares for your peals? I peal too; and I tell you I won't be imposed on. Here, Elizabeth; I have got ye a husband, at last, to my heart's content.

MISS DOILEY
Him, sir! You presented that gentleman to me this morning, and I have found such a fund of merit in him—

DOILEY
In he! what, in that beau-bookworm! that argufies me down, I don't know English? Don't go for to provoke me; bid that Mr Granger welcome to my house; he'll soon be master on't.

MISS DOILEY
Sir, in obedience to the commands of my father—[Significantly.]—

DOILEY
Sha'n't say obedience; say something kind to him of yourself.—He's a man after my own heart.

MISS DOILEY
Then sir, without reserve, I acknowledge, your choice of Mr Granger is perfectly agreeable to mine.

DOILEY
That's my dear Bet!

[Kissing her.

We'll have the wedding directly. There! d'ye understand that, Mr Tri-Pantry?—is that English?

GRADUS
Yes, so plain, that it has exsuscitated my understanding. I perceive I have been duped.

DOILEY
Aye, well! I had rather you should be the dupe than me.

GRADUS

Well, sir, I have no inclination to contest, if the lovely Charlotte will perform her promise.

CHARLOTTE
Agreed! provided that, in your character of husband, you will be as singular and old-fashioned as the wig you wore this morning.

DOILEY
What, cousin! have you taken a fancy to the scholar? Egad, you're a cute girl, and mayhap may be able to make something of him; and I don't care if I throw in a few hundreds, that you mayn't repent your bargain. Well, now I've settled this affair exactly to my own mind, I am the happiest man in the world. And, d'ye hear, Gradus? I don't love for to bear malice; if you'll trot back to college, and larn the difference between Greek and English, why, you may stand a chance to be tutor, when they've made me a grandfather.

GRADUS
I have had enough of languages. You see I have just engaged a tutor to teach me to read the world; and if I play my part there as well as I did at Brazen-Nose, your indulgence will grant me applause.

[Exeunt.

Hannah Cowley – A Short Biography

Hannah Cowley was born Hannah Parkhouse on March 14th, 1743, the daughter of Hannah (née Richards) and Philip Parkhouse, a bookseller in Tiverton, Devon.

As one might expect details of much of her life are scant and that of her early life almost non-existent.

However, we do know that she married Thomas Cowley in either 1768 or 1772 and that the marriage produced 3 or perhaps 4 children.

The couple moved to London after their marriage and Thomas worked as an official in the Stamp Office and as a part-time journalist.

Her career in the literary world seemed to happen rather late. It was whilst the couple were attending a play, thought to be sometime in late 1775, that Cowley was struck by a sudden necessity to write. "So delighted with this?" she boasted to him. "Why I could write as well myself!"

And she set to work. By the next day she showed him the first act of her comedy; The Runaway. She set about finishing the rest of the play and then sent it to the famed actor-manager, David Garrick. It was produced at his final season at the Drury Lane theatre on February 15th, 1776.

The Runaway enjoyed 17 performances in its first season at Drury Lane and was revived many times thereafter.

Its initial success, and the encouragement of the newly retired Garrick, ensured that Cowley would write more. She wrote her next two plays, the farce, Who's the Dupe? and the tragedy, Albina, before the year was out.

Who's the Dupe? and Albina encountered several difficulties getting into production. The new manager of Drury Lane, Richard Brinsley Sheridan, postponed The Runaway for most of the 1777 season. Upset, Cowley thought of an alternate means to get her play produced. She sent Albina to Drury Lane's rival theatre in London, Covent Garden. Alas it was not accepted. Albina now bounced back and forth between the two theatres for the next two years. Meanwhile, Sheridan agreed to produce Who's the Dupe? but the premiere would only take place in the spring, an unprofitable time for a new play to open.

The play brought controversy. Her rival Hannah More had written Percy and it opened in 1777. Cowley thought several parts of it were similar to her own, as yet, un-produced play. It raised her suspicions. When Hannah More next had The Fatal Falsehood open in 1779 Cowley was convinced that More had plagarised from her own Albina.

Indeed when The Fatal Falsehood opened on May 6th, 1779, it was followed by charges in the press that More stole her ideas from Cowley. On August 10th, More wrote to the St. James Chronicle to protest that she "never saw, heard, or read, a single line of Mrs. Cowley's Tragedy." Cowley herself was hurt but acted with good grace. She wrote in a later printed preface to Albina that hers and More's plays do indeed have "wonderful resemblances." And she allowed that theatre managers, who in those days also acted as script editors, may have inadvertently given More her ideas: "Amidst the crowd of Plots, and Stage Contrivances, in which a Manager is involv'd, recollection is too frequently mistaken for the suggestions of imagination"

Albina finally opened on July 31st, 1779, at the Haymarket to neither financial nor critical success.

With the Hannah More controversy behind her, Cowley wrote her most popular comedy, The Belle's Stratagem. It was staged at Covent Garden in 1780. In its first season it performed for 28 nights and was regularly revived helping to ensure a solid revenue stream for Cowley and her family.

Her next play, The World as It Goes; or, a Party at Montpelier (the title was later changed to Second Thoughts Are Best) was unsuccessful, but she continued to write and there followed another seven plays; Which is the Man?; A Bold Stroke for a Husband; More Ways Than One; A School for Greybeards, or, The Mourning Bride; The Fate of Sparta, or, The Rival Kings; A Day in Turkey, or, The Russian Slaves and The Town Before You.

Sadly, none could recreate her initial triumph.

In 1783, Thomas Cowley accepted a job with the British East India Company and left for India leaving his wife in London to continue her career and to raise their children. Thomas never returned to England and died in India in 1797.

As well as plays Cowley also wrote poetry. In 1786, she wrote "The Scottish Village, or Pitcairne Green".

In 1787, under pseudonym "Anna Matilda," she and the poet Robert Merry (under his own pseudonym of "Della Crusca") began a poetic correspondence through the pages of The World journal. The poems were sentimental and flirtatious. Initially they did not even know the others' identity; but they later met and became part the Della Cruscans poetry movement. This volume of poetry was published under her pseudonym in 1788 as The Poetry of Anna Matilda.

Cowley's last play, The Town Before You, was produced in 1795.

In 1801 Cowley published perhaps her greatest poetical work. A six-book epic "The Siege of Acre: An Epic Poem".

That same year Cowley retired to Tiverton in Devon, where she spent her remaining years out of the public spotlight whilst she quietly revised her plays.

In her day, Cowley's works were popular and thought provoking. One critic noted she was "one of the foremost playwrights of the late eighteenth century" whose "skill in writing fluid, sparkling dialogue and creating sprightly, memorable comic characters compares favourably with her better-known contemporaries, Goldsmith and Sheridan."

Hannah Cowley died of liver failure on March 11th, 1809.

Hannah Cowley – A Concise Bibliography

Plays
The Runaway (1775, Staged 1776)
Who's the Dupe? (1776, Staged 1779)
Albina (1776, Staged 1779)
The Belle's Stratagem (1780)
The World as It Goes; or, a Party at Montpelier
Which is the Man?
A Bold Stroke for a Husband (1783)
More Ways Than One
A School for Greybeards, or, The Mourning Bride
The Fate of Sparta, or, The Rival Kings
A Day in Turkey, or, The Russian Slaves
The Town Before You (1795)

Poetry
The Scottish Village, or Pitcairne Green (1786)
The Poetry of Anna Matilda (A pseudonym) includes A Tale for Jealousy and The Funeral (1788)
The Siege of Acre: an Epic Poem (1801)

Scenarios of Some of Her Plays

The Runaway (1776)

George Hargrave, who is home from college, is overjoyed to learn that Emily, the mysterious runaway whom his godfather, Mr. Drummond, has taken in, is the same young lady he fell in love with at a recent masquerade. Meanwhile, George's spirited cousin, Bella, helps George's sister, Harriet, and George's friend Sir Charles fall in love. George's designs are threatened when he learns that his father wants George to marry Lady Dinah, a pretentious older lady who is also very rich. When Emily's father arrives to take Emily back to London, George gives chase and snatches Emily back. Mr. Drummond saves the day by offering the young lovers some of his land so that they can have a fortune of their own.

Who's the Dupe? (1779)

Granger, a captain, arrives in town to see his lover, Elizabeth. Her uneducated father, Abraham Doiley, has promised her hand to the most educated man he can find, an unappealing but intelligent scholar named Gradus. Elizabeth's friend Charlotte, who fancies Gradus for herself, persuades Gradus to act more fashionable and less bookish so that he can win Elizabeth's heart. Doiley is not impressed by the new Gradus; meanwhile, Granger presents himself to Doiley as a scholar so that he can win Elizabeth's hand. Granger and Gradus square off against each other to see who is the more educated, and Granger wins by using phony Greek that nonetheless impresses Doiley. Gradus is consoled by winning Charlotte.

Albina (1779)

The powerful Duke of Westmorland learns that the gallant young soldier Edward is in love with his daughter, Albina, who is a young widow to Count Raimond. Despite her love for Edward, Albina's virtue impedes her from agreeing to marry him. Westmorland and Edward persuade her to remarry because Edward is soon destined to go off to war; she agrees. Editha, who is jealous of Albina, seeks help from Lord Gondibert, Raimond's brother, who secretly loves Albina. On the eve of the wedding, Gondibert tells Edward that Albina has been unfaithful, and to prove it he disguises himself and allows Edward to spy on him sneaking into Albina's chamber at night. Edward then calls off the wedding, and the furious Westmorland challenges him to a duel to protect Albina's honour. Before the duel begins, Gondibert's elderly servant, Egbert, exposes his master's lie, and the king banishes Gondibert. Before he leaves, Gondibert vows to kill Albina and then commit suicide. He sneaks into Albina's chamber and stabs a woman he thinks is Albina, and then he stabs himself. But the woman turns out to be a disguised Editha, who had also stolen into the room. Edward is relieved when the real Albina rushes into the room, and the dying Gondibert asks for and receives her pardon.

The Belle's Stratagem (1780)

Having returned from his trip to Europe, the handsome Doricourt meets his betrothed, Letitia. He finds her acceptable but by no means as elegant as European women. Determined that she will not marry without love, Letitia enlists the help of her father, Mr. Hardy, and Mrs. Racket, a widow, to turn Doricourt off the wedding by pretending that she, Letitia, is an unmannerly hoyden. Meanwhile, Doricourt's friend Sir George is being overprotective of his new wife, Lady Frances, who rebels and agrees to accompany Mrs. Racket for a day in the town and a masquerade ball that night. While out at an auction, Lady Frances meets the rake, Courtall, who brags to his friend Saville that he will seduce her. Meanwhile, Letitia's brazen acting succeeds in dissuading Doricourt from wanting to marry her. All characters converge at that night's masquerade. The disguised Letitia shows off her charms, bewitches Doricourt and then leaves before he can find out who she is. Courtall, disguised the same way as Sir George, lures the lady he thinks is Lady Frances back to his house. However, Saville has replaced the real Lady Frances with a prostitute who is disguised as Lady Frances is. Shamed, Courtall leaves town. The next day, Doricourt, who has been told that Mr. Hardy is on his deathbed, visits him and reluctantly agrees to marry Letitia after all. Then the disguised Letitia enters and reveals her true identity to the overjoyed Doricourt, who also learns that Hardy was not ill after all.

A Bold Stroke for a Husband (1783)

Set in Madrid, the play tells of Don Carlo, who has fled his wife, Victoria, for the courtesan Laura. Laura breaks off with Don Carlo, but she holds on to the documents that entitle her to his land, a gift he foolishly gave her. We learn that Laura is in love with Florio, who is really Victoria disguised as a young man. Meanwhile, Victoria's friend Olivia is resisting efforts by her father, Don Caesar, to marry her off to a series of suitors. In desperation, Don Caesar pretends that he will marry and young girl and then send Olivia off to a convent unless she marries right away. Victoria persuades Olivia's servant to disguise himself as her rich uncle, the original owner of the land that Laura now holds. He convinces Laura that the titles are worthless, so in a rage she rips them up. Victoria reveals herself to Don Carlos, who repents and pledges himself to her again. Meanwhile, Olivia gets married to Julio, the man she wanted all along.

www.ingramcontent.com/pod-product-compliance
Lightning Source LLC
Chambersburg PA
CBHW060103050426
42448CB00011B/2600